HAMPSTEAD DOWNSTAIRS/THE PETER WOLFF TRUST PRESENTS

AND NO MORE SHALL WE PART

By Tom Holloway
Directed by James Macdonald

Cast:
Dearbhla Molloy
Bill Paterson

Creative Team:
Designer **Hannah Clark**
Lighting Designer **Guy Hoare**
Sound Designer **Christopher Shutt**
Production Manager **Matt Noddings**
Stage Manager **Erin Murphy**
Technical Assistant Stage Manager **Cressida Klaces**
Head of Production **Tom Nickson**
Set Construction **Ben Leveson**
Line Producer **Lucy Jackson**

CAST

Dearbhla Molloy Pam

THEATRE: *Cripple of Inishmaan* (Druid, USA Tour); Beatrice in *Much Ado* (Guthrie Theatre, Minneapolis); *In Celebration* (Wyndham's); *Arcadia* (Haymarket); *The Hostage, Lovegirl and the Innocent* (RSC); *Hinterland, On the Ledge* (National Theatre); *Juno and the Paycock* (Donmar); *Ditch* (Old Vic Tunnels); *Pieces of Vincent* (Arcola); *Aristocrats, Translations, Ivanov, Mrs Warren's Profession, The Misanthrope* (Abbey Theatre Dublin); *Phaedre, Uncle Vanya, The Philanthropist, Come On Over* (Gate Theatre Dublin). **BROADWAY:** *A Touch of the Poet, Dancing at Lughnasa, Juno and the Paycock* (Roundabout NY); *Cripple of Inishmaan* (Atlantic Theatre NY). **FILM AND TELEVISION:** Numerous credits in Britain, Ireland and the U.S. **AWARDS:** Two Drama Desk Awards, Theatre World Special Award, London Critics Award, Two Irish Theatre Awards, Audie Award. Nominations: Tony Award, Royal Television Society Award, Independent Film and Television Award, Grammy Award.

Associate Artist of the Abbey Theatre, National Theatre of Ireland.

Bill Paterson Don

THEATRE: *Earthquakes in London, The Marriage Play, Good Person of Scezhuan, Schweyk in the Second World War* and *Guys & Dolls* (National Theatre); *Ivanov* (Almeida Theatre); *Misery* (Criterion); *Death & The Maiden* (Royal Court/Duke of Yorks); *Crime and Punishment* (Lyric, Hammersmith); *A Man with Connections* (Royal Court/Traverse); *And Me Wi' A Bad Leg* (Royal Court); *Whose Life Is It Anyway* (Savoy Theatre); *Ella* (ICA); *Writer's Cramp* (Hampstead/Bush); *Treetops* (Riverside); *A Mongrel's Heart* (Royal Lyceum); *Little Red Hen* (7:84 Theatre Co.); *The Cheviot, The Stag & The Black Black* Oil (7:84 Theatre Co.); *The Games a Bogey* (7:84 Theatre Co.); *Great Northern Welly Boot Show* (Edinburgh Festival); *Willie Rough* (Royal Lyceum). **TELEVISION INCLUDES:** *Doctor Who, The Forgotten Fallen, Law and Order UK, Little Dorrit, Criminal Justice, Sea of Souls, Danielle Cable: Eye Witness, Wives and Daughters, Melissa, The Crow Road, Traffik, The Singing Detective, Auf Wiedersehen Pet, Smiley's People, The Cherry Orchard, The Vanishing Army, Licking Hitler, The Cheviot, The Stag & The Black Black Oil.* **FILM INCLUDES:** *Miss Potter, Bright Young Things, Hilary and Jackie, Richard III, Truly Madly Deeply, The Adventures of Baron Munchausen, The Witches, Defence of The Realm, A Private Function, Comfort & Joy, The Killing Fields.* **RADIO INCLUDES:** *Tales from the Back Green,* his own series for radio, was published in 2008.

Bill is a Fellow of The Royal Conservatoire of Scotland.

CREATIVE TEAM

Tom Holloway Writer

Tom is an award-winning Australian playwright. Plays include *Beyond The Neck* (Performing Lines, Tasmania, 2008 – winner of the Australian Writers Guild award for Writing For The Stage); *Don't Say The Words* (Griffin Theatre Company and Tasmania Theatre, 2008); *Red Sky Morning* (Red Stitch Actors Theatre, 2008 – Green Room Award for Best New Australian Play); *And No More Shall We Part* (Griffin Theatre Company, 2011 Winner of the Australian Writer's Guild for Writing For The Stage and the Louis Esson Victorian Premier's Award For Literature) and *Love Me Tender* (Company B Belvoir St/Griffin Theatre Company and Thin Ice, 2009 & 2010); *Gambling* (Soho Theatre/Eleanor Lloyd Productions, London 2010); *Fatherland* (The Gate Theatre, London 2011 and Munich Yung Og Radikal Festival). In 2006/2007 Tom was one of ten writers whose work was selected to be presented as part of the Royal Court Theatre's International Young Writers Festival. Tom received the Max Afford award in 2010 for his new work *Faces Look Ugly* and is currently under commission to the Bell Shakespeare Company and the Melbourne Theatre Company and is writing a new play for the Liverpool Everyman and Belvoir Street Theatre in a UK/Australia co-commission. Tom's libretto as part of a new opera, *Make No Noise* was performed at the Munich Opera Festival in summer 2011.

James Macdonald Director

THEATRE: *Cock* (Off-Broadway, Duke Theater); *King Lear, The Book of Grace, Drunk Enough to Say I Love You* (the Public Theatre); *A Delicate Balance, Judgment Day, The Triumph of Love* (Almeida); *John Gabriel Borkman* (Abbey Theatre Dublin/BAM); *Cock, Drunk Enough to Say I Love You, Dying City, Fewer Emergencies, Lucky Dog, Blood, Blasted, 4.48 Psychosis* [including European/US tours], *Hard Fruit, Real Classy Affair, Cleansed, Bailegangaire, Harry and Me, Simpatico, Blasted, Peaches, Thyestes, The Terrible Voice of Satan* (all for the Royal Court); *Dido Queen of Carthage, The Hour We Knew Nothing of Each*

Other, Exiles (NT); Top Girls (Broadway/MTC); *Glengarry Glen Ross* (West End); *Dying City* (Lincoln Center); *A Number* (New York Theatre Workshop); *Troilus und Cressida, Die Kopien* (Berlin Schaubühne); *4.48 Psychose* (Vienna Burgtheater); *The Tempest, Roberto Zucco* (RSC); *Love's Labour's Lost, Richard II* (Royal Exchange, Manchester); *The Rivals* (Nottingham Playhouse); *The Crackwalker* (Gate); *The Seagull* (Sheffield Crucible); *Miss Julie* (Oldham Coliseum); *Juno and the Paycock, Ice Cream and Hot Fudge, Romeo and Juliet, Fool for Love, Savage/Love, Master Harold and the Boys* (Contact Theatre); *Prem* (BAC/Soho Poly). **OPERA:** *A Ring A Lamp A Thing* (ROH Linbury); *Eugene Onegin, Rigoletto* (WNO); *Die Zauberflöte* (Garsington); *Wolf Club Village, Night Banquet* (Almeida Opera); *Oedipus Rex, Survivor from Warsaw* (Royal Exchange/Hallé); *Lives of the Great Poisoners* (Second Stride). **FILM:** *A Number* (HBO/BBC). Associate Director of the Royal Court from 1992 – 2006. NESTA fellow 2003 – 2006.

Hannah Clark Designer

Hannah trained at Central School of Speech and Drama. She was a winner of the 2005 Linbury Biennial Prize for stage design. Designs include: *Motor Show* (Requardt & Rosenberg); *Angus, Thongs and Even More Snogging* (West Yorkshire Playhouse); *The God of Soho, As You Like It* and *A Midsummer Night's Dream* (Shakespeare's Globe); *Pericles* (Regent's Park Open Air Theatre); *Episode, Roadkill Café, Pequenas Delicias,* and *Jammy Dodgers* (Frauke Requardt & Company); *The Talented Mr Ripley* and *Under Milk Wood* (Northampton Theatre Royal); *Behud* and *Gambling* (Soho Theatre); *Eigengrau* and *2nd May 1997* (The Bush); *The Boy on the Swing, Light Shining in Buckinghamshire, Knives in Hens, Thyestes* and *Torn* (Arcola); *Be My Baby* (Derby Live); *Nocturnal* and *Big Love* (The Gate); *Bunny* and *Terre Haute* (Nabokov); *Billy Wonderful* (Liverpool Everyman); *The Snow Queen* (West

Yorkshire Playhouse); *Company* and *Hortensia and the Museums of Dreams* (RADA); *Proper Clever* (Liverpool Playhouse); *House of Agnes* (Paines Plough); *Breakfast with Mugabe* (Theatre Royal Bath); *As You Like It* and *We That Are Left* (Watford Palace Theatre); *The Cracks in my Skin* and *Who's afraid of Virginia Wolff?* (Manchester Royal Exchange); *Othello* (Salisbury Playhouse); *Wuthering Heights* (Aberystwyth Arts Centre & tour); *Death of a Salesman, What the Butler Saw, Blue/Orange, A View from the Bridge, I Just Stopped By To See The Man*, and *Two* (Bolton Octagon); *The Taming of the Shrew* (Bristol Old Vic).

Guy Hoare Lighting Designer

THEATRE: *Future Proof* (Traverse & Dundee Rep); *Peter Pan* (National Theatre of Scotland); *A Doll's House* (Young Vic); *In Basildon* (Royal Court); *Be Near Me; Serenading Louie* (Donmar); *A Delicate Balance; Waste* (Almeida); *Othello* (West End); *Electra* (The Gate); *Faith Healer* (Bristol Old Vic); *A Christmas Carol;* (Birmingham Rep); *Annie; As You Like It; Macbeth* (West Yorkshire Playhouse); *Kes* (Liverpool Playhouse); *Amadeus; Assassins; Fen, Far Away* (Sheffield Theatres). **DANCE:** *The Metamorphosis* (ROH2/Arthur Pita); *The Land of Yes, The Land of No* (Sydney Dance Company); *Square Map of Q4* (Bonachela Dance Company); *Frontline* (Aterbaletto); *Pavlova's Dogs* (Scottish Dance Theatre); *Dream* (NDCWales); *And Who Shall Come to the Ball?* (Candoco); *The Lessening of Difference, About Around* (bgroup); *Mischief* (Theatre Rites); *Made In Heaven, Love & War; Sea of Bones, Bad History, Green Apples; Dive* (Mark Bruce Company); *White Space; Second Signal; Shot Flow* (Henri Oguike Dance Company); *Bruise Blood, Flicker* (Shobana Jeyasingh Dance Company). **OPERA:** *Jakob Lenz* (ENO); *The Cunning Little Vixen* (Brno); *The Barber of Seville, La Clemenza di Tito, Gianni Schicchi, Il Tabarro, Fantastic Mr Fox, Promised End, The Duenna, The Magic Flute, Katya Kabanova, Don Giovanni, Anna Bolena, Susannah, The Seraglio, Eugene Onegin* (ETO).

Christopher Shutt Sound Designer

THEATRE: *War Horse, Piaf, The Caretaker, Humble Boy, Shoes* (West End); *Comedy of Errors, Emperor and Galilean, Beyond the Horizon/Spring Storm, The White Guard, Burnt by the Sun, Every Good Boy Deserves Favour, The Hour We Knew Nothing of Each Other, Happy Days, Coram Boy* (National Theatre); *Playboy of the Western World, All About My Mother, A Moon for the Misbegotten* (Old Vic); *Disappearing Number, Elephant Vanishes, Mnemonic, Street of Crocodiles* (Complicite); *School for Scandal, Julius Caesar* (Barbican); *Ruined, Judgement Day* (Almeida); *Prince of Homburg, The Man Who Had All the Luck, Hecuba* (Donmar Warehouse); *Kin, Aunt Dan and Lemon, Free Outgoing, The Arsonists, Road, Serious Money* (Royal Court); *Blasted* (Lyric Hammersmith); *Good* (Royal Exchange, Manchester); *Twelfth Night, The Tempest, King Lear, Romeo & Juliet, Noughts & Crosses, King John, Much Ado About Nothing* (RSC); *The Bacchae, Little Otik* (National Theatre of Scotland); *Riders to the Sea* (ENO); *War Horse, All My Sons, Happy Days, King Lear, A Moon for the Misbegotten, Not About Nightingales, Mnemonic, Resistible Rise of Arturo Ui* (Broadway). **RADIO INCLUDES:** *Shropshire Lad, Maud, After the Quake.*

Tony Award for *War Horse* on Broadway. New York Drama Desk Awards for *War Horse, Not About Nightingales* and *Mnemonic.* 4 Olivier Award Nominations.

Lucy Jackson Line Producer

Lucy is an independent producer and project manager. Theatre includes *Mudlarks* (HighTide Festival Theatre) *Fanta Orange, Don Juan Comes Back From the War*, the *Vibrant – A Festival of Finborough Playwrights* festivals (Finborough Theatre); *Amphibians* (Bridewell Theatre); *Phillipa and Will are Now in a Relationship, The Sexual Awakening of Peter Mayo* (Pleasance Edinburgh/ Theatre503); *The Folk Contraption* (VAULT Festival/ London Wonderground/Latitude Festival); *White Rabbit, Red Rabbit* (Volcano Theatre/Remarkable Arts); *Thom Tuck Goes Straight-to-DVD* (Fosters Edinburgh Comedy Award Nominee for Best Newcomer 2011).

Hampstead Theatre would like to thank:

The Revolving Stage Company
Soho Theatre
Royal and Derngate Theatres
Elly Hopkins
Kate McDowell

Supported using public funding by
**ARTS COUNCIL
ENGLAND**

And No More Shall We Part was first presented as part of the Hampstead Downstairs season of new writing in January 2012.

It transferred to the Traverse Theatre, Edinburgh in August 2012 as part of the Edinburgh Festival Fringe.

This production has been licensed by arrangement with Casarotto Ramsay and Associates Ltd.

Hampstead Theatre

Hampstead Theatre is one of London's most vibrant theatres, where many renowned theatrical personalities have begun their careers.

Our completely flexible Main House has a real epic dimension: it is the perfect home for robust, resonant and enriching plays. We work with the world's most prominent Theatre-Makers to create productions of the very highest standard for the broadest possible audience. With new plays at the heart of the programme we present work that is refreshingly unfamiliar – bold and relevant, yet always entertaining. We are therefore perfectly positioned to make a unique and important contribution to British Theatre.

Hampstead Downstairs

'The Theatre Downstairs at Hampstead is one of the most exciting interventions into the new writing theatrical landscape in London for the past five years. Here is a space which is bravely experimental. It has the bravery to live without the approval of critics. It allows writers and actors and directors to work with honesty and daring. It allows them the right to experiment. It is intimate and intense. In the space of a year it has become essential.' – **Simon Stephens**, award-winning playwright and Artistic Associate of the Lyric Hammersmith. His play *The Trial of Ubu* had its UK Premiere at Hampstead Theatre in January 2012.

Hampstead Downstairs was created as a response to feedback from playwrights, regarding the lack of opportunities to stage new plays. Presenting New Writing is intrinsically high risk and there are very few places where writers can hone their craft.

The programme enables writers from a wide variety of backgrounds and experiences to trial new work in our studio, without the pressures of commercial interests or theatre critic reviews, but with a paying audience who have the opportunity to offer feedback. The aim is to identify and develop plays which might have the potential to move to our Main Stage or to larger stages elsewhere.

In opening up our studio space with a professional series of work for the first time, Hampstead Downstairs has become an indispensible part of the new writing ecology in just 18 months. We have increased capacity and supported new writers, whilst substantially improving the quality of new writing.

'"Skåne" had been sitting around for well over a year before I heard that Hampstead Theatre wanted to stage it. I was excited and relieved that what Ed, Will, Greg and others in the building, felt they had read on the page, could work on stage. I'm very grateful for their imagination and faith in my writing, and they do such a great job of making you feel welcome and valued. Thank you. The insistence that I work with an established director and not someone I know was daunting but they were very patient

in finding one whose approach would most suit me and my play. And I loved working with Tim Carroll. I've learned a lot from Tim's process, particularly how his actors come to the performance through the text, which, in turn, is influencing how I come to and hear dialogue in my writing currently. With no pressure to perform for reviews, the work felt... well, all about the work...a rare experience in this business, I think, and I was and will remain very proud of the production.' – **Pamela Carter**, writer of *Skåne*, produced in the Hampstead Downstairs Programme in November 2011.

'Working in the studio allowed me to take time to construct the world of Tom Holloway's difficult and subtle play – and the actors to develop complex characterisation – over time, organically, without the constraints on the process which are normally imposed [in British theatre at least] by the swift tumbril ride towards a press night. It seems to me that what the studio project has the potential to do is to change the ecology of presenting new work in British theatre, but it's tricky to make this change, and unsurprisingly there are plenty of vested interests who would prefer change not to happen. Here too the answer is time – the project simply needs to keep going for its virtues and its successes to become clear to a wider public, and for the whole dialogue between a theatre and its potential audience to cut out the middlemen.' – **James Macdonald**, director of *And No More Shall We Part*.

'I may have said this before but Downstairs at @Hamps_Theatre is my favourite theatre at the moment. The quality is exceptional.' (Twitter comment about the Hampstead Downstairs programme in 2011/12).

'The Studio is an exquisite place to work in. Removing press nights means that work made there can be genuinely experimental, engaging for practitioners and audiences alike. The space itself is utterly flexible and beautifully intimate.' – **Katie Mitchell**, director of *small hours*, Hampstead Downstairs, January 2010.

Hampstead Theatre is grateful to the following Trusts for their invaluable support of the Downstairs programme:
The Andor Charitable Trust
The Columbia Foundation Fund of the Capital Community Foundation
The Fenton Arts Trust
The Idlewild Trust
The Leche Trust
The Rayne Foundation
The Peter Wolff Trust

AND NO MORE SHALL WE PART

Tom Holloway

AND NO MORE SHALL WE PART

OBERON BOOKS
LONDON

WWW.OBERONBOOKS.COM

First published by Currency Press Pty Ltd, 2011
PO Box 228, Strawberry Hills, NSW 2012 Australia
www.currency.com.au

First published in the United Kingdom in 2012 by Oberon Books Ltd
521 Caledonian Road, London N7 9RH
Tel: +44 (0) 20 7607 3637 / Fax: +44 (0) 20 7607 3629
e-mail: info@oberonbooks.com
www.oberonbooks.com

A catalogue record for this book is available from the British
Library.

ISBN: 978-1-84943-502-4

Printed and bound by CPI Group (UK) Ltd, Croydon, CR0 4YY.

Visit www.oberonbooks.com to read more about all our books
and to buy them. You will also find features, author interviews and
news of any author events, and you can sign up for e-newsletters
so that you're always first to hear about our new releases.

Characters

PAM
56-year-old woman

DON
61, Pam's husband

And No More Shall We Part was first produced by A Bit of Argy Bargy and Full Tilt for the Melbourne Fringe Festival at Black Box Theatre, Melbourne, Australia on 30th September 2009.

And No More Shall We Part received its UK premiere at the Hampstead Downstairs, London on 12th January 2012 with the following cast:

PAM   Dearbhla Molloy

DON   Bill Paterson

Creative Team

Writer, Tom Holloway

Director, James MacDonald

Designer, Hannah Clark

Lighting, Guy Hoare

Sound, Christopher Shutt

SCENE ONE

We see PAM and DON. PAM is in a single bed. DON is sitting in a chair next to it.

There is a long silence.

DON: Anything?

PAM: No.

DON: Really?

PAM: Sorry.

DON: Right.

PAM:

    PAM looks at DON in the chair.

DON: What?

PAM: Do you remember when we went to the beach?

DON: Sorry?

PAM: Do you?

DON: I don't…

PAM: Years ago.

DON: Really?

PAM: Yes. With the kids. Do you remember that?

DON: I…

PAM: To go camping. It was spring I think. Remember?

DON: Oh. When they were little?

PAM: Yes.

DON: Right. Perhaps.

PAM: I was just thinking about it.

DON: Really?

PAM: Mmm.

DON: I'm not sure I really remember. Sorry.

PAM: Right.

DON:

PAM: It was spring but still not really warm enough. Actually cold. Actually it was still very cold. But they wouldn't let up. They hounded us about it.

DON: That sounds…

PAM: Over and over. Can we go? Can we go? And we told them. It's too cold. It's still too

DON: Oh, yes!

PAM: But they wouldn't listen. Pester power.

DON: Of course!

PAM: So we went. Drove out to. Where was it?

DON: Oh…

PAM: Where was…

DON: Where on Earth was

PAM: Anyway. We went. Pitched the tents. Set up camp. Right near the beach. Lit a fire and set up camp. The family out there. All together.

DON: Yes.

PAM: And it was bloody awful.

DON: Yes!

PAM: You remember?

DON: Terrible!

PAM: It was so

DON: Absolutely

PAM: It was even colder than we'd thought!

DON: Yes!

PAM: The wind!

DON: It's coming back to me now!

PAM: And the kids. Suddenly they hated it. Well, we thought… They screamed and wailed. Wouldn't go near the water. Didn't want to leave the car even.

DON: No!

PAM: God, they could be so frustrating.

DON: Could be?

PAM: I was just thinking. I remember when we were there. Sitting huddled together. All of us. In our sleeping bags. Outside, but each in our sleeping bags. The second night it was. And the sun had long. You know. Long gone. And it was cold and dark and so, so windy. And you had tried valiantly

DON: Valiantly?

PAM: Yes. Valiantly.

DON: That sounds like me.

PAM: My prince.

DON:

PAM: You had tried valiantly to get a fire going but everything was so wet. The wood and things. Wet from a winter's worth of rain and things. And Billy. He was, what? Five?

DON: That sounds right.

PAM: And he says. No sings! Out of the blue!

DON: Yes!

PAM: He sings those lines from the Turtles song!

DON: Yes, of course!

PAM: We're all huddled from the cold. And the wind. That terrible icy wind and he sings 'we're happy together'

DON: Yes!

PAM: 'So how is the weather'!

DON: Yes!

PAM: The Turtles!

DON: Yes! He did! That's right. God, how do you remember these things?

PAM: And the look on his face. In his eyes. In the light from the gas lamp. He's shivering and blue. Basically blue. Like we all are. Huddled in our sleeping bags. But he looked so happy! Turned and looked so happy at all of us and sang that. Let alone where a five-year old learns the words to songs from the Turtles! And he had to basically shout it over the wind and we all looked at each other and just

DON: Yes!

PAM: Broke out laughing. Hysterically.

DON: God, yes!

PAM: So hard we

DON: Yes, hurt!

PAM: Yes! All of us.

DON: My God…

PAM: So we packed everything up right then. Laughing and joking. In the dark. Jumped back in the car. Headed home. Got back in the middle of the night.

PAM: What a little trip it was, remember?

DON: Yes.

PAM: The laughter. The joy of it.

DON: That's right.

PAM: Remember?

DON: It was great.

PAM: Wasn't it?

DON: God, yes.

PAM: And we got back. Came back here. Hot showers and heating and our own beds. You know? At. I don't know. One or Two in the morning probably. All having showers and washing and saying good night. We put them to bed and then sat here. Like this. I was in bed already and you sat there in that chair. Just like this. Just like this now.

DON: Yes. That's right.

PAM: I mean in the other room. In our bedroom. Your bedroom.

DON: Ours.

PAM: But still, just like this.

DON: Ours, Pam.

PAM: And do you remember what you said? Sitting in that chair as you took your shoes off and got ready to get in. Do you?

DON: I…

PAM: Do you remember?

DON: I'm not…

PAM: You told me you loved me. I love you, you said. I still love you like in the beginning. You said that to me. Out of the blue you said that.

DON: Right.

PAM: And you gave me this look.

DON: Oh yes?

PAM: Yes.

DON: What look?

PAM: Like you wanted me. Like how you looked at me in the beginning.

DON: Right.

PAM: I love that look.

DON: Right.

PAM: Can you give it to me now?

DON: What?

PAM: The look. Can you look at me like that now?

DON: What, just

PAM: Yes.

DON: Sorry, I don't…

PAM: But can't you? I mean considering, you know? Can't you?

DON: Don't say that.

PAM: But

DON: I mean, how? How can I? I don't even know what you're. What look you're

PAM: You don't?

DON: They're not. Those kind of things. They're not things you can just do, you know?

PAM: I know. Sorry. I just thought…

DON:

PAM: Can you remember why? What made you say that? At that moment? Out of the blue like that?

DON: Back then?

PAM: Yes.

DON: Well, it was true.

PAM: But what made you? Right then? Can you remember?

DON: Well, because it was

PAM: No I mean. What it was. In that moment. Can you?

DON: I… no. Sorry.

PAM: You can't?

DON: No.

PAM: Oh.

DON: I can't even remember saying it actually.

PAM: Really?

DON: No.

PAM: Really?

DON: Sorry.

PAM: Right.

DON:

PAM: I often think about that. That's all. That moment. And now you're sitting there, so it's like it again. In a way. You don't remember?

DON: Sorry.

PAM: No. It's okay.

DON:

PAM: How funny that was.

DON: Yes.

PAM:

DON: It's still true though.

PAM: Sorry?

DON: I do still love you. Just the same.

PAM: Please.

DON: I do though.

PAM:

DON: I still look at you exactly the same. I still feel exactly
the same about you.

PAM: Wrinkles and all?

DON: Yes. Wrinkles and all.

PAM:

DON: You know that, don't you?

PAM: Yes.

DON: I love you Pammy. I love you with. Well. I don't know what I. What I will

PAM: Stop.

DON: But I don't

PAM: Stop, please.

DON: I might not be able to give you a look, but… I mean

PAM: It's

DON: I mean I really don't know what I'm going to…

PAM:

DON: Sorry.

PAM:

DON:

PAM: Why did we stop going camping?

DON: What?

PAM: Why did we ever stop? It used to be so much fun.

DON: Yes.

PAM: So, why did we?

DON: I don't know.

PAM: Hmm.

DON: Adolescence probably.

PAM: Yes. Probably.

DON: Who wants to go camping with your parents when you can hang around with your friends doing… god knows what.

PAM: Exactly.

DON: Yes.

PAM: Pity though.

DON: Yes.

PAM:

DON: Should we go now?

PAM: Don.

DON: Pack up the car? Pull the old tent out. Take off?

PAM:

DON: Right.

PAM:

DON:

DON: Are you all right?

PAM:

DON: How are you feeling?

PAM: I don't

DON: Anything?

PAM: I can't tell. Not yet I think.

DON: Right.

PAM:

DON: Want a cuppa or something? A cup of tea?

PAM: I shouldn't.

DON: Might help.

PAM: No.

DON: Right.

PAM:

DON:

PAM: I wish I could just fall asleep, you know?

DON:

PAM: God. Normally I'm out like a light. This would all be so much easier if I could just fall asleep.

DON: Pam, I…

PAM:

DON: Sorry.

PAM:

DON: So. You're not tired at all?

PAM: No. Well, a bit perhaps. But not enough to, you know. Actually sleep.

DON: Right. And nothing else? You're not feeling anything else?

PAM: Not really.

DON: Should you? By now?

PAM: I'm not sure.

DON: How long ago was it?

PAM: Twenty minutes perhaps? Maybe more. Something like
       that?

DON: Right.

PAM: But I don't know. We never looked into how long it
       would take to kick in.

DON: We should've done that.

PAM: Yes. Maybe.

DON:

PAM:

DON: Pam.

PAM: Sorry?

DON: Maybe I should. I was thinking maybe I should do it
       too.

PAM: What?

DON: Maybe I should do it too.

PAM: Don!

DON: Because

PAM: No! Stop! Don't say that!

DON: But

PAM: God!

DON: We could. Together.

PAM: Stop!

DON: But

PAM: Stop!

DON: Sorry.

PAM: We can't… you can't.

DON: But

PAM: Don.

DON: No.

PAM:

DON: Sorry.

PAM: Please, don't say that.

DON: No.

PAM: God.

DON: It's just

PAM: Don. I know, but…

DON:

PAM:

DON:

PAM: I'm glad they're not here.

DON: What?

PAM: The kids.

DON: Pam…

PAM: But I couldn't. Not knowing they were just through the wall.

DON: I know, but...

PAM: I mean what would they. What would they be doing?

DON: Sorry?

PAM: The kids?

DON: Oh. I'm not sure. Pottering I guess.

PAM: Right.

DON: TV or something.

PAM: Right. You think?

DON: Maybe.

PAM: Maybe they'd be bunked down.

DON: I doubt it.

PAM: Maybe they'd be asleep already?

DON: I doubt it. I mean how could they?

PAM: I suppose. But it would be funny wouldn't it? If they were sound asleep while I'm in here buzzing at a hundred miles an hour.

DON: Yes.

PAM: They'd probably start banging on the wall, asking me to keep it down.

DON: Probably.

PAM: Like we used to do to them.

DON: Yes. With their music and things.

PAM: Keep it down up there!

DON: Yes.

PAM: We're trying to sleep!

DON: Or something like that. TV. We're trying to watch TV!

PAM: Yes. So can you keep it down up there?!

DON: Yes.

PAM: Can you just hurry up and die up there already!

DON: Pam!

PAM: Sorry.

DON:

PAM: But it's a bit like that, isn't it?

DON:

PAM: Sorry.

DON:

PAM:

PAM: Do you think I took them correctly?

DON: Of course you did.

PAM: But, I mean…

DON: You'd gone over the instructions a hundred times.

PAM: In the right order?

DON: Yes. I'm sure you would have.

PAM: Did I take enough? Maybe I didn't take enough.

DON: You took what you were told to, yes? You did everything like you were told to. I don't know why you're not feeling... Why nothing is

PAM: Right.

DON: Jesus, this is. This is so

PAM: Darling.

DON: But this is. It's crazy isn't it? Isn't this crazy?

PAM: Don.

DON: This whole thing is completely

PAM: Don, I've taken them. You can't say this now.

DON: But nothing is happening! Why isn't anything happening!

PAM: I don't know.

DON: Surely by now. Surely after this long something should be

PAM: Don.

DON: But something should be

PAM: Stop Don.

DON: But

PAM: Stop. It must. I don't know. It must just take a bit of time. That's all.

DON: But I can't

PAM: Yes you can.

DON: No, Pam. I can't.

PAM: You have to Don.

DON: Why?

PAM: Why?

DON: Yes, why?

PAM: Don. You have to.

DON:

PAM: You have to. You know that.

DON:

PAM: It must just take time.

DON:

PAM: It's just going to take a bit of time.

DON: We did everything right. We followed the instructions.

PAM: So it must just take a bit of time. Okay?

DON: You don't feel anything?

PAM: Darling.

DON: Sorry. I'm sorry.

PAM: I know.

DON: It's just

PAM: I know.

DON: Jesus.

PAM:

DON: Look at me getting all worked up.

PAM: My prince.

DON: I don't feel like it.

PAM: My chambermaid then.

DON: That's more like it.

PAM: Yes.

DON: Sorry.

PAM:

DON: We'll just wait.

PAM: Yes.

DON: Sorry.

PAM: This is the right thing, Don.

DON: I know.

PAM: This is what I want.

DON: I know.

PAM: So…

DON: Yes.

PAM: My love.

DON:

PAM:

DON: I might. I might just go and give them a call.

PAM: What?

DON: The kids. Just a quick call.

PAM: No Don.

DON: But

PAM: You can't.

DON: They'll want to know how you are though.

PAM: Don…

DON: I won't be long. Just a moment. Ring the bell if you.
      You know. Need anything.

PAM: You can't call them Don.

DON: But I need

PAM: I know, but

DON: I mean, I need to

PAM: Don. This is best.

DON: They don't care about… I don't care about

PAM: I know. But, still…

DON: Pammy…

PAM: Please?

DON:

PAM: My love?

DON: How did I ever let you talk me in to this?

PAM: Pester power.

DON: I'm going to be alone.

PAM:

DON: Aren't I?

PAM: Yes. For a little bit.

DON: I don't know how I'm going to…

PAM:

DON: Yes. Well I… I've got to go to the toilet anyway. My bladder…

PAM: Yes. Has a mind of its own.

DON: I'll make a run for it then. Ring the bell if you need me. And don't die while I'm on the loo, okay?

PAM: I'll try not to.

DON: God.

PAM: Don't call them. Please?

DON:

PAM: My prince.

End of scene.

SCENE TWO

Weeks earlier. We see DON and PAM at home. PAM comes in, unnoticed by DON. She goes up to him and looks over his shoulder at the newspaper he is mulling over.

PAM: Reconcile.

DON: What?

PAM: That's the word.

DON: What? Oh. Oh it is! You can't do that!

PAM: Sorry.

DOM: That is mean!

PAM: I just saw it.

DON: That is just mean!

PAM: Sorry.

DON: I've been staring at if for an hour, you walk in and just see it!

PAM: It happens sometimes, you know that.

DON: I know. But you didn't have to tell me!

PAM: Sorry.

DON: If I did that to you

PAM: You're right.

DON: You know?

PAM: I'd be ropeable. Yes. You're right.

DON: Yes you would.

PAM: Sorry, I couldn't stop myself.

DON: That would be right.

PAM:

DON: Are you okay?

PAM: What?

DON: You seem a bit…

PAM:

DON: Oh. You're back!

PAM: Yes.

DON: Back from the

PAM: Yes.

DON: Right.

PAM:

DON: So…

PAM:

DON: How was it?

PAM: Sorry?

DON: What did they say?

PAM: Oh. Right.

DON: Well?

PAM: Can I have. Do you mind making me a cup of tea?

DON: But

PAM: I've just walked in the door. Can I just have a moment
to relax?

DON: But what did they

PAM: Don.

DON: Say?

PAM: Please?

DON: What?

PAM:

DON: Okay. A cuppa then. Okay.

PAM: Thank you.

DON: Right.

DON goes to the kitchen and turns the kettle on. PAM sits down.

While DON is away, PAM sits alone. It is for a few minutes. In silence.

We hear the kettle whistle. PAM is still alone.

DON comes back in with two cups of tea.

PAM: They're ending treatment.

DON: What?

PAM: They told me they're going to stop treatment.

DON: Who said that?

PAM: Don…

DON: The doctors? Doctor What's-his-face?

PAM: Yes. Doctor What's-his-face.

DON: No!

PAM: They

DON: Why?

PAM: They said

DON: But, why?

PAM: Because

DON: No.

PAM: Yes.

DON: No!

PAM: Don.

DON: But why are they stopping it?

PAM: Because it's not

DON: But there's months to go. There's so much of it still to

PAM: Yes, but

DON: Stopping it?

PAM: Yes.

DON: But that means

PAM: Yes.

DON: It means

PAM: I know.

DON: But surely there's still. I mean there should be so much more to go. Surely it might

PAM: They don't think so.

DON: No. No that's crazy! That's

PAM: Please Don.

DON: But that's unfair! They can't just! Not now. Not like this!

PAM: Please.

DON: They don't get. They don't understand what

PAM: Yes they do.

DON: No!

PAM: They're specialists Don. This is what they do. They know what they're. They know what's best for me.

DON: Best?

PAM: Yes.

DON: Doctor What's-his-face knows what's best?

PAM: Stop pretending you don't know his name. He's been my doctor for three years now.

DON: This isn't best! How can this be

PAM: Because

DON: But how can this be best?

PAM: Because I can't go through it.

DON: What?

PAM: The treatment. If it's not helping, I can't keep doing it.

DON: But it is helping.

PAM: No.

DON: It must be. That's what it does. It helps.

PAM: Not for me.

DON: This is. We'll go somewhere else. We'll get other specialists. I never liked the look of him anyway. Down at us. He always looked down at us! This is not how it's going to

PAM: Don

DON: We'll get a second opinion. Better. We'll go to someone better! I've never liked him or those other doctors anyway.

PAM: Don. Can I have

DON: No Pam. This is not how it's

PAM: Can I have my tea?

DON: I'm not going to just give up like this. I'm not. We're not.

PAM: Can I just

DON: I can't believe they would do that. That he would say that. Ending it? Ending treatment? There's no reason why we should

PAM: Don

DON: No Pam! There's no reason why we should just give up like that!

PAM: Please, give me my tea.

DON: Why should we just give up like that?!

PAM: Please?

DON: No!

PAM: Stop!

DON:

PAM:

DON: Here you go.

PAM: Thank you.

He gives her her tea and also sits down.

DON:

PAM:

DON: God.

PAM: Yes.

DON: This means…

PAM: Yes.

DON:

PAM: We need to talk about this.

DON: Yes.

PAM: No. There's something I think we need to talk about with this.

DON: Yes, I know Pam.

PAM: No Don.

DON: I'm not ready to just

PAM: No Don. You're not listening.

DON: Sorry?

PAM: I want to talk to you about something.

DON: What?

PAM: I want to talk to you about something. To do with all this.

DON: What do you mean?

PAM: You need to. Will you promise to hear me out?

DON: What do you mean?

PAM: Can you promise you'll hear me out with what I'm about to say?

DON: Hear you out?

PAM: Not get carried away?

DON: What are you talking about?

PAM: Just. Can you promise to let me finish what I have to say and not get carried away? Not get worked up?

DON: Pam. What are you

PAM: Can you?

DON: I don't know what you're

PAM: I'm going to get very sick Don.

DON: Sorry?

PAM: They're ending treatment. You know what that means. We know what is going to come now.

DON: But

PAM: Please. So, I'm going to get very sick and then I'm. This is certain now, okay? This is for certain. I will get very sick. Be in a great deal of pain. Helpless. Needing immense help for basic. For very basic. The money. The pain. What it will do to you. To the kids. To Mel and Billy. And then I'm going to die.

DON: Pam, don't say

PAM: Let me finish, please. We need to talk about this.

DON: But they shouldn't end the treatment! We need to get a second opinion!

PAM: No.

DON: Because, ending treatment? Now? This early? That's

PAM: Don. I want them to.

DON: What?

PAM: I agree with them. I want to end it. I can't do it any more.

DON: You can't do it?

PAM: No.

DON: But

PAM: So please, listen to me.

DON: What's this about Pam?

PAM: I'm going to get very sick. We've both read about what's going to happen. It's going to be. I mean what I have in front of me is...

DON: Pam?

PAM: It's going to be horrible Don. For me and for you. It's going to be truly

DON: Yes. But. I mean. We're not there yet, are we? We're not

PAM: Yes we are.

DON: No! Come on! You're overreacting! We're not at that point yet, are

PAM: I've been doing research. I asked someone about it.

DON: About what?

PAM: About how I can end it.

DON:

PAM: Don?

DON:

PAM: Donny?

DON: End it?

PAM: Yes.

DON: Pam?

PAM: Before I get too sick.

DON: End it?!

PAM: Yes.

DON: What?

PAM: Don.

DON: But, what?

PAM: I

DON: You asked someone?

PAM: Yes.

DON: Who?

PAM: It's best I don't. I shouldn't tell you who.

DON: Shouldn't tell me?

PAM: No.

DON: What do you mean, you shouldn't

PAM: Legally.

DON: What?

PAM: It's best I don't tell you who because of legal reasons.

DON: Legal?

PAM: Yes.

DON: Oh my god. What are we talking about here? What is going on here?

PAM: And it's hard, it won't be easy, but

DON: Jesus!

PAM: But I can get a combination of. Of pills. Not technically legally. But I can.

DON: Pills?

PAM: Yes.

DON: This is. This is crazy!

PAM: Don.

DON: No.

PAM: We need to

DON: No!

PAM: But

DON: A minute or two ago Pam. Just a minute or two ago you were ruining my target word. And now we're. Now you're talking about…

PAM: Yes.

DON: And I'm not supposed to get. You don't want me to get carried away? To get upset?!

PAM: Please, Don?

DON: No.

PAM: Please?

DON: No! I can't talk about this!

PAM: We have to.

DON: No we don't!

PAM: There's two sets of pills I need. The ones that will. You know. Do it. And

DON: Do it?

PAM: And the ones that will help me keep the other ones down.

DON: God!

PAM: That will stop me throwing them up.

DON: Pam. I love you. I. Don't do this. Don't say these. Don't do this!

PAM: I have to Don.

DON: No. I can't. I can't listen to

PAM: We have to talk about it.

DON: No. I won't! This is not the way to. We're not there yet. We're nowhere near to that point yet.

PAM: Yes we are.

DON: No!

PAM: Yes I am.

DON: NO!

PAM:

DON: NO!

DON stands. He is about to leave.

PAM: What are you doing?

DON: I'm not going to sit here and listen to this.

PAM: Please Don. You promised me.

DON: No I didn't.

PAM: Please, we need to.

DON: You can't do this to me. You can't talk about this.
Leaving me? You want to leave me? And I should just
sit here and be happy with it?

PAM: Leave you?

DON: Yes Pam. Leave me. That's what you're saying.

PAM: No.

DON: Yes!

PAM: Don. I can't. It's too much. I can't do it. I don't want to go out like

DON: Go out?

PAM: Die like that.

DON:

PAM: Please?

DON: This is crazy.

DON walks out.

PAM: Don!

PAM is left alone. She drinks her tea.

End of scene.

SCENE THREE

Back in the present. PAM is in bed. Her eyes are closed and she doesn't move. DON enters.

He sees PAM.

DON: Pam?

PAM:

DON: Pam!

PAM: What?

DON: Oh. God. I thought

PAM: Sorry. I was lost in my thoughts.

DON: You scared me.

PAM: Did you call?

DON: No.

PAM: Thank you.

DON: Don't say that.

PAM:

DON: Are you getting tired?

PAM: A little.

DON: I was thinking. What about some sleeping pills? Just to help start. Just so you can go to sleep.

PAM: I don't know.

DON: I know the notes said not to take anything else, but

PAM: I don't think we should.

DON: But it's been. It must have been forty-five minutes by now.

PAM: Just sit with me.

DON: But

PAM: Just sit back down and talk to me. Maybe I can go to sleep to your voice. Tell me a story or something.

DON: Story?

PAM: Yes.

DON: I don't…

PAM: Just sit and talk to me.

DON sits back down.

    I might not talk much. Might not answer. But I'm listening. Okay?

DON: What should I talk about?

PAM: I don't know.

DON: And you'll just drift off?

PAM: Hopefully.

DON: And…

PAM: Yes.

DON: Pammy.

PAM: A story?

DON: But…

PAM: I know, Don.

DON:

PAM: A story then.

DON: Well…

PAM: Something to leave me with.

DON: Pam…

PAM: Yes.

DON: I mean…

PAM:

DON: What kind of…

PAM: Just something to help me drift off to.

DON: You do seem more tired.

PAM: Yes. I guess.

DON: I don't know what to tell you.

PAM: Something lovely.

DON: Pam, I…

PAM: Please?

DON: I don't

PAM: Tell me what you're going to do this time next week.

DON: What?

PAM: Or next month. Once this is. Once it's just you. After everything has settled down and it's just you.

DON: No. I can't. I can't talk about

PAM: But you'll be okay, won't you?

DON: No. No I won't be okay.

PAM: Please Don.

DON: I can't talk about that. I can't.

PAM: Then something else. Anything. Just talk while I lie here.

DON: You don't. I don't know how you can be like this. So calm. During this. You're always so calm whenever anything. While I fly off the handle, you always stay so… how do you do that?

PAM: It's not easy.

DON: Who's going to be calm for me now? Who's going to be the one to bring me back to Earth now?

PAM: I don't know.

DON:

PAM: You'll have to do it yourself.

DON: Yeah right.

PAM: Good luck with that.

DON: Yeah. Thanks.

PAM:

DON: Right. A story then. Or something.

PAM:

DON: Right.

PAM:

DON: Okay. I don't know if I ever told you this. I don't think I have. When I was a kid. Very young. Six or seven. Something like that. This is so silly. I can't believe this is what I'm deciding to tell you about now. Right now.

PAM: Just tell me.

DON: Okay.

PAM:

DON: So I was about six or seven I think. Something like that. I remember at school. In class. We were learning about minerals and things. You know? Fool's gold and real gold. Crystals. All that kind of thing. And I remember the teacher telling us about diamonds. She had one. On a ring. It must have been her engagement ring or something. I've never thought about it, but I guess it was probably her engagement ring. That's probably why we had the whole class. The whole lesson. So she could tell all us kids about her diamond ring. Hmm. Anyway. I remember her telling us how diamonds are formed. How they're carbon, you know? Tightly compacted carbon that has turned in to diamond deep in the ground. I didn't know what carbon was so I asked. Coal, she told me. Said it was basically coal. Like in the fire. Like wood after a fire. I remember I couldn't believe it. I couldn't believe that that stuff sitting in the fireplace at home was where diamonds came from. She told us how valuable diamonds were. How expensive they were. Probably also to show off hers. But I just thought, how could something so valuable come form something so, I don't know. Dead? You know?

PAM:

DON: And then I had a thought. I can't believe I thought this. For lots of reasons I can't believe it. But it's always stayed with me. Maybe because it was one of the first times I had, I don't know, a revelation. Something like a revelation. Although what a silly… I thought I could do it myself. Make a diamond. I got an old ice cream container or something. I don't remember. I went to the fireplace and got out a big piece of coal. Bigger than my hand. If I was going to make a diamond I might as well make a big one. So I got it out and put it in the container and went out in to the garden. I filled the container with dirt, packed it as tightly as I could. Put the lid on. Then I dug a hole and buried it. Just near the clothesline. I tried burying it as deeply as I could. By the end of it I was covered in dirt and soot. And I thought, when I'm old. When I'm an old man. Because I knew it took a long time. So I thought when I'm an old man I'm going to go back there and dig it up and. I really thought this. Give the diamond to my family. To my kids. And they'd be rich. I can't believe I thought that. I mean not just how stupid it was. How I clearly hadn't really understood what we'd been told in class. But that I was something like six and already planning for my family. That's the thing that really gets me. I can't believe I was thinking like that at that age. And now here I am. An old man. I've got a family. I've got you and Billy and Mel and… How funny that is. How… and look at us now. Look at what we're doing now?

PAM:

DON: Pam?

PAM:

DON: Pam, are you…

PAM:

DON: Pam?

PAM:

DON:

PAM: You've told me that before.

DON: Jesus!

PAM: What?

DON: I thought you had…

PAM: I know. Sorry. I keep drifting off in my thoughts.

DON: Jesus!

PAM: Sorry.

DON: This isn't. Something should be happening Pam.

PAM: Something is. I don't know what. But something is. I'm getting more tired I guess.

DON: I don't know. I don't like it. It doesn't feel right.

PAM: You've told me that before. That story.

DON: What?

PAM: When you gave me my ring. Remember?

DON: Did I?

PAM: Yes.

DON: Right.

PAM: You never remember anything, do you?

DON: What?

PAM: You told it to me then.

DON: Of course. Sorry. I forgot.

PAM:

DON: I can't even get. Jesus, I can't even get that right, you know? The last story.

PAM: It's okay.

DON: No it's not.

PAM: It really is Don.

DON: But

PAM: My prince. My wonderful…

DON:

PAM: My…

DON: What should we do?

PAM: I don't know.

DON: Does it feel right, to you?

PAM: I'm not sure.

DON: Do you think this is how it should be?

PAM: I don't know.

DON:

PAM: Maybe I should just. Maybe you should just go to bed and I could read.

DON: What?

PAM: I always go to sleep when I read.

DON: Go to bed?

PAM: Yes.

DON: No.

PAM: It's probably the best idea.

DON: I don't want to go to bed. How could I go to

PAM: I'm not going to be able to sleep with you sitting there like that. Sitting over me like that.

DON: Over you?

PAM: Yes.

DON: Pammy…

PAM: And. You know. Things are happening now. I can feel something. So it's probably best for you not to be here. So you don't have to lie more than you already do.

DON: I don't care about

PAM: Don.

DON:

PAM: I'll just read and drift off and you can come in and find me in the morning and call the doctor and things. That's probably the best thing to do. The most natural. You know?

DON: I know, but. But leaving you?

PAM: Yes.

DON: But that means…

PAM:

DON: Pam?

PAM: Yes. Sorry. I know what that means. How about you just kiss me on the forehead and say good night and head off to bed?

DON: Pammy. My Pammy. I...

PAM: I know Don. We've said it all before. It's okay. Really.

DON: Oh god.

PAM:

DON: Right.

PAM:

DON: Well, I guess this is it.

PAM: Yes.

DON: Right.

PAM: Good night then, my prince.

DON: Chambermaid.

PAM: Yes.

DON: Pam...

PAM:

DON: Right.

> *DON leans in and kisses PAM on the forehead.*

Good night then.

PAM: Night.

DON: I…

PAM: Yes. Turn the light off as you go, please?

DON: Right.

PAM: Thanks.

DON: Night then.

PAM: Good night.

> *DON hesitates and then leaves the room, turning off the main light as he goes. In the bedside light we see PAM reach for her book and open it, but she doesn't get to read. Not in this moment that we see.*

> *End of scene.*

SCENE FOUR

Weeks earlier. We see PAM.

PAM: JESUS!

   DON rushes in.

DON: What?

PAM: Jesus Christ!

DON: What is it? Are you okay?

PAM: Jesus, this… this whole thing is… Jesus Christ!

DON: What is it Pam? What's wrong?

PAM: I can't do this! I can't go on like this!

DON: Pammy?

PAM: All I wanted… I just wanted some marmalade!

DON: Sorry!

PAM: I just wanted to have some bloody marmalade, for Christ's sake!

DON: Marmalade?

PAM: Is that so weird?!

DON: You hate marmalade Pam.

PAM: I just wanted to have a bit of marmalade on toast and there isn't any! There isn't any in the whole bloody house!

DON: Pam?

PAM: Jesus Christ! Is that too much… is marmalade too much to ask for?

DON: But Pam, you hate marmalade. We both do. I don't understand.

PAM: I hate it, do I?!

DON: Yes. I think so. You always have.

PAM: What would you know about what I want and what I don't?

DON: Pammy?

PAM: Or did you just not buy it to try to control me or something? Was that it?

DON: What?

PAM: You're not the boss of me, Don.

DON: I'm not? I know I'm not. What... please, Pammy, what is this about?

PAM pulls a pamphlet out of her pocket.

PAM: What's this?

DON: What?

PAM: This pamphlet that was in the kitchen.

DON: Oh.

PAM: I found it when I was looking for marmalade.

DON: Right.

PAM: With whom have you been talking?

DON: With whom?

PAM: Yes.

DON: No one.

PAM: What, you just leave this lying around? Just like that?

DON: I thought this was about marmalade.

PAM: Because you can't just say it? You can't just come out
       and say it?

DON: You can't tell me what

PAM: You can't say it to my face so you leave this lying
       around?

DON: Well, so what if that is what I was doing? I don't want
       us to do this, Pam. I don't want you to

PAM: Where did you get this from?

DON: St Peters.

PAM: What?

DON: The church. The local

PAM: You've been going to church?!

DON: I didn't talk to anyone. I just

PAM: Since when do you go to church?!

DON: Pam, you know I was brought up a

PAM: What?

DON: I mean I went to a Catholic school for Christ's sake!

PAM: Because you went to catholic school, you're now all of a sudden going to the local church?

DON: What I do, Pam. Is... is my...

PAM: Your business?

DON: Yes. What I do is my business.

PAM: While I'm stuck in this house you're going off to church and bringing dirt like this back in to our home?

DON: Well you haven't given me a say in what you're doing, so...

PAM: I what?

DON: I don't want to do this. I think this is wrong. Very wrong. I'm sorry, but

PAM: I'm dying Don.

DON: Don't play that.

PAM: Play that?

DON: No.

PAM: Don, I'm... I mean... I'm bloody dying! I'm going to bloody die! You've got no... I mean you've go no idea what that is... what I have to... Look at me. I can't even… if I don't. If we don't do this. In 6 months I will be… less maybe. You want to go through that?

DON: It's wrong.

PAM: You want me to go through all that pain?

DON: There are drugs. Palliative care.

PAM: Palliative care?

DON: Jesus Pam, you never asked me what I… I've at no point had any say in any of this!

PAM: Ask you?

DON: Yes! Ask me what I think! How I'm feeling about all this! You're so… you're…

PAM: What?

DON: So selfish!

PAM: Selfish?

DON: Yes!

PAM: How dare

DON: This isn't just about you. This is about me too. This is about us.

PAM: About you? About us?

DON: Yes!

PAM: Jesus!

DON: I'm sorry, but

PAM: How dare you. How dare you do this! Look at me! Look at what's happening to me! I'm dying! I'm going to...

DON: I know, but

PAM: No you don't!

DON:

PAM: I will never see the kids get married. I will never meet their husband or wife. I'll never get to meet my grandchildren. I mean, my grandchildren! I'll never get to hug Billy again or go for lunch with Mel. I'll never get to read a book. To see a film. I'm never going to get to do any of that and you're going to get to do all of that and I'm being selfish?

DON:

PAM: Or you. I'll never get to hold you again. To touch you.

DON:

PAM: Don?

Long silence.

DON: I had an affair. Fifteen years ago.

PAM: I know.

DON: How?

PAM: Sal told me.

DON: Your sister?

PAM: She knew the woman somehow.

DON: Really?

PAM:

DON: But you never said…

PAM: I had one too.

DON: You did?

PAM: To get back at you. It was horrible. I hated it.

DON: Me too.

Long silence.

We have to tell the kids.

PAM: What?

DON: I think we need to tell the kids.

PAM: About…

DON: Yes.

PAM: No.

DON: Pam, we can't

PAM: But legally, Don. If they know then they can be held, you know, they can be arrested. It's bad enough I told you.

DON: Who cares? They're our children and they have to know.

PAM: But, for them. To make sure they're safe. Because this is. You know. What we're going to do is illegal Don.

DON: And I think it should be too.

Silence.

PAM: Where have you been, anyway?

DON: I was on the computer.

PAM: The computer? You?

DON: I heard someone. Down at the club. They said you could get target word problems off the newspaper sites.

PAM: And now all of a sudden you need to tell the kids.

DON: I looked it up.

PAM: What?

DON: I did some research. On the computer. On the Internet. We don't have to do it like this at least.

PAM: What do you mean?

DON: I'm not trying to talk you out of it. That was stupid. And I deleted my searches. I called Mel and asked her how to do that. There's a place. In Switzerland. We can do it properly. It will be legal and

PAM: I don't want to go to Switzerland. I want to do it here. In our home.

DON: I know Pam. But doing it here. Doing it your way. On the information you got from. From whoever it was. There's so much risk involved. It could go wrong and

PAM: It won't.

DON: How do you know?

PAM:

DON: But, you know. Going means. We can do it properly.
      The kids can come. They can be part of it. Like it
      should be.

PAM: You hate the Swiss. Boring. You've always said you
      thought they were boring.

DON: So what?

PAM: So why would we go there to do this?

DON: Because they can help us.

PAM: I've got help.

DON: But like this Pam? Doing it like this?

PAM: I'm sorry. I know this is hard. All this. The whole. But I
      don't want to

DON: Well I don't want to do this at all! I don't want any of
      this! I do think this is wrong! I do think I should get a
      say in it and I do think you're being bloody selfish and
      I do think you want to leave me!

PAM:

DON: I've told the kids.

PAM: What?

DON: A few days ago. Well actually, Billy asked. It seems a few years ago you mentioned something to him about it. That if you ever got sick you thought you'd do this. He seemed to think you'd said that to him.

PAM: Oh.

DON: So I've told them what you're planning to do.

PAM: Me?

DON: Yes.

PAM: You shouldn't have done that Don. Without talking to me.

DON: Well I did it. And they want to be involved.

PAM: I thought it would just be you and me. I was okay thinking about it when it was just you and me.

DON: On the website they said there were stages they put you through. Questions and things. To test you. To make sure you're sure. Just look at this. Them being involved. As one of those. A test. Because I don't want to. I won't do this if you're not one hundred percent sure Pam. I just can't.

PAM: To test me?

DON: Yes.

PAM: You want to test me?

DON: So. The kids. They're going to be involved. Both of them.

PAM: Bloody catholic.

DON: We'll eat together. As a family. And they'll be here. That's how it's going to be. Okay? A last meal together. If we do this.

PAM: This is what I want Don.

DON: I know.

End of scene.

SCENE FIVE

The present. We see DON. It is the middle of the night. He is in pajamas. He has a pillow and blanket with him.

He goes up to the door to PAM's room. He goes to open the door but then decides not to.

He sits there on the floor for a long moment.

He lays out the pillow, puts the blanket over him and tries falling asleep, with his hand on the door.

End of scene.

SCENE SIX

The final dinner. We see PAM. She is sitting at a set dining table, waiting. After a while DON enters with a bag. The table is only set for two.

DON: Got it.

PAM: Right.

DON: Can't believe I forgot ice cream.

PAM: Yes.

DON: Those two, it's like they're still 6 years old whenever they come here for dinner.

PAM: Isn't it?

DON: Gotta have ice cream. You could. You know. Be making the most exquisite… most exotic thing they've ever… but still there has to be ice cream at the end of it all.

PAM: They're their father's children.

DON: That they are.

PAM: It's funny that even now they're not home, you always buy two-litre containers of it for one little meal.

DON: Well, you know…

PAM: Yes.

DON: Can't let it go to waste.

PAM: Of course.

DON: So…

PAM: My little ice-cream man.

DON: That's me.

PAM: Yes.

DON: Did you keep your eye on the oven for me?

PAM: Of course.

DON: Am I back before the timer?

PAM: That, you are.

DON: Right. Good.

PAM:

DON: They're not here yet?

PAM: No.

DON: Right. I thought they would be by now. You know. Considering everything.

PAM: Yes.

DON: Still probably just, I don't know, traffic or

PAM: Don.

DON: What?

PAM: Don. They're not coming.

DON: Sorry?

PAM: They're not

DON: What do you mean, they're not

PAM: I

DON: Coming?

PAM: I asked them

DON: They have to come.

PAM: No. No they

DON: Yes. You asked them what?

PAM: Not to.

DON: You asked them not to?

PAM: Yes.

DON: What do you mean?

PAM: It's for the

DON: Best?

PAM: Yes. It's for the best.

DON: No it's not.

PAM: Don.

DON: I said, Pam. I told you. If we were to do this then the last... the... then we would all eat together first. One last dinner together first.

PAM: I know, Donny.

DON: That was all I asked for.

PAM: I know.

DON: So. I'm sorry. But I'm going to call them and they are going to come over or we're not going to

PAM: Don.

DON: No, Pam.

PAM: I talked to them. I've seen them already today and I talked to them. Said, you know, our goodbyes. They agreed that tonight should just be

DON: Jesus!

PAM: Just be you and me.

DON: You've seen them already?

PAM: Yes. Earlier today.

DON: Without me?

PAM: Yes.

DON: Why?

PAM: Because I needed to

DON: What about. Sorry Pam. But what about what I need?

PAM: I know. I'm

DON: What about me in all this?

PAM: I'm sorry Don. I think it's. I know this is hard. But it's for the best. It's really

DON: Bullshit!

PAM: What?

DON: Bullshit!

PAM: What did you say?

DON: I'm sick of that. Of hearing that. For the best. I'm sick of it!

PAM:

DON: This is. This whole thing is…

PAM:

DON throws the ice cream at the wall.

DON!

DON: What?

PAM: Please!

DON: What?

PAM:

DON: I'm sorry.

PAM:

DON: I'm…

PAM:

DON: God. I didn't even realize how you'd set the table.

PAM: You and me.

DON: What am I going to do Pammy?

PAM: I've talked to them. The kids. They're going to take it in turns. Being here with you. Over the next month at least. A week at a time or whatever.

DON: What?

PAM: Starting tomorrow.

DON: They're going to…

PAM: As soon as you call them, once it's… once we've…

DON:

PAM: So I've seen them. I got to tell them what I wanted to and not. That's not something everyone gets to do. I'm lucky to get to… to say those things to them. You

know? And now you and I shall sit down and eat the
delicious meal you've been making and we'll, well, you
know what we'll do.

DON: I wanted us all to be…

PAM: I know.

DON: I wanted one last time of us all together.

PAM: I know. It would have been lovely. But we can't.

DON: Why not?

PAM: You know why not.

DON:

PAM: So. Can we eat together my darling?

DON:

PAM: It smells delicious.

DON: I don't think there'll be any ice cream for desert.

PAM: No. Probably not.

We hear a timer go off in the other room.

There we go.

DON: Pammy?

PAM: Yes?

DON:

PAM: Not too much for me. I shouldn't have too full a
      stomach, remember?

*DON doesn't answer. He goes in to the kitchen. After a long pause he
brings out two plates of food, puts one in front of PAM and the other
plate at the other set place.*

      Thank you. It looks wonderful.

DON: Wine. Should I get some

PAM: Probably not. Not for me anyway.

DON: Right.

PAM: Are you going to sit with me?

DON: Yes.

PAM: Can I have a little. A bit of a kiss from the chef?

DON: Sorry?

PAM: Can I?

DON: Oh. Right.

DON goes and gives PAM a kiss on the forehead before sitting down opposite her.

PAM: Thank you.

DON:

They sit and eat in silence.

Halfway through eating his meal, DON breaks down. PAM lets him cry and keeps eating. After a while he wipes the tears from his face and also continues eating.

PAM finishes her meal. DON leaves the rest of his.

PAM: Delicious.

DON: Do you want more?

PAM: No.

DON: Are you sure?

PAM: Yes.

DON: How are you feeling?

PAM: I'm good.

DON: Right.

PAM: A little tired.

DON: Really?

PAM: Yes.

DON: Right.

PAM: What a delicious meal.

Long silence.

I think. Maybe I should take the pills now.

DON: What?

PAM: I think this would be a good time to

DON: Already?

PAM: I think so.

DON: But don't you want to… can't we…

PAM: Maybe you should clear the plates and while you're putting them in the dishwasher I can sit here and take them and then you can help me to bed?

DON: But Pammy…

PAM: Can you help me, my love?

DON: But…

PAM: Because I have to take them alone, you know.

DON:

PAM: You could clear up and then come here. Hold out your
       arm to help me up and then escort me to my bedroom.
       What do you think about that?

DON:

PAM: My love?

*After a long pause DON stands, collects the plates and walks to the
kitchen. Just before he leaves the room he says…*

DON: Pam.

PAM: Yes?

DON: I…

PAM: Yes.

DON goes in to the kitchen.

*PAM gets a pillbox out of her pocket. She places it down in front of
her. She looks at it for a long moment.*

She opens the box and takes the first pills. It is a struggle to swallow them.

She takes the second pills. Again it is difficult to get them down.

She sits alone with the empty pillbox in front of her.

After another pause, DON walks back in and sees the empty box. He walks over to PAM. He puts his arm out for her to use to help her stand. She is surprisingly weak, but from the disease, not the pills.

Once she stands she breaks down. She hugs him while she cries, and he holds on to her tightly. This is held for a long time.

After a very long moment like that, she lets go and stands on her own.

Right.

DON: Pam?

PAM: Take me to the bedroom then.

DON:

She hooks her arm in to his and they walk out of the room.

End of scene.

SCENE SEVEN

The present. Morning. We see PAM's room. She is not in bed. We hear a bell tinkling in the room. DON enters.

DON: Pam?

He sees she's not there. He goes to the side of the bed.

Pam! God! Are you okay?

He rushes over and leans down. PAM is on the ground. We can't see her.

Oh god, oh god. Pam? Pam?

He tries picking her up and putting her back in bed. It is very difficult for him. She has vomited and it is on her face, in her hair and on her clothes. She doesn't move much. Finally he gets her in to bed.

Pam!

He tries cleaning her face.

Pam, are you… are you okay? Please! Please be okay! Please!

PAM stirs.

Oh god. Pammy. My Pam. What happened? I'm sorry. I'm so. God, I'm so sorry!

PAM: Wha…

DON: It's okay. I'll call... I'll call the doctor.

PAM: Don?

DON: I get the doctor. Jesus. Oh, god...

PAM: It didn't work Do...

DON: What?

PAM: I don't think it wor...

DON: Oh god. Just lie here. Just lie still. I'll call the doctor.

PAM: It didn't wor...

DON: I'll get the doctor.

PAM: Maybe I should've. Maybe I... I should... should've taken...

DON: Don't talk. Don't. It will be okay. Don't...

PAM: I want to be... I don't... I want... Don. I don't want to be. I want to...

DON: I know Pammy.

PAM: I... I vomited. I... Don? Don?

DON: I'll call the doctor.

PAM: No.

DON: What?

PAM: No… no doc…

DON: But, Pam! But you're

PAM: No doc…

DON: Jesus! Jesus, this is! My Pammy. My darling. I'm so…

PAM: Don?

DON: Yes?

PAM: No doc… We can't…

DON: Oh, Pam…

PAM: Don?

DON: Don't talk.

PAM: But…

DON: Jesus!

PAM:

DON: Right. No doctor. Right. I'm here for you Pam. I love
you. Pam… Oh Pammy…

PAM:

*DON lies on the bed next to PAM, holding her, stroking her hair.
He is getting vomit on his hands but he doesn't stop. They lie there
together. Close. He is almost spooning her in the single bed. Nothing
more is said.*

End of play.

'Together we have something and share a passion
that other people will never understand'

Mark and Angela are a father and daughter grappling with a
painful past and fragile future. Tonight, an innocent evening of
ice cream and DVDs derails quickly into dangerous territory
in this chilling new story about a father who loved too deeply.

'a powerful piece of experiential theatre with
a heart-stopping climax'
Aleks Sierz, *The Stage*

'a play of great power, both subtle and shocking…complex
and challenging'
Anna Winter, *New Statesman*

9781849430449

WWW.OBERONBOOKS.COM